A Garland Series

The English Stage
Attack and Defense 1577 - 1730

A collection of 90 important works
reprinted in photo-facsimile in 50 volumes

edited by
Arthur Freeman
Boston University

Commonwealth Tracts
1625-1650

85911

with a preface
for the Garland Edition by

Arthur Freeman

Garland Publishing, Inc., New York & London

1974

Library of Congress Cataloging in Publication Data
Main entry under title:

Commonwealth tracts, 1625-1650.

(The English stage: attack and defense, 1577-1730)
    Reprint of the 1625 ed. of A shorte treatise against
stage-players; of the 1641 ed. of The stage-players
complaint, printed for T. Bates, London; of the 1642 ed.
of A declaration of the Lords and Commons assembled in
Parliament, for the appeasing and quietting of all unlawfull tumults and insurrections ... also an ordinance of
both Houses, for the suppressing of stage-plays, printed
for J. Wright, London; of the 1643 ed. of The actors
remonstrance, or complaint ... printed for E. Nickson,
London; of the 1647 ed. of Two ordinances of the Lords
and Commons assembled in Parliament, printed for
R. Ibbitson, London; of the 1647 ed. of An ordinance of
the Lords and Commons assembled in Parliament, for, the
utter suppression and abolishing of all stage-playes
and interludes, imprinted for J. Wright; London; of the
1647 ed. of The dagonizing of Bartholomew Fayre; of the
1650 ed. of To the supreme authoritie, the Parliament of
the Common-wealth of England. The humble petition of
diverse poor and distressed men, heretofore the actors
of Black-Friers and the Cock-pit.
    1. Theater--England--History--Sources. I. Series.
PN2592.C6   1974   792'.0942   71-170417
ISBN 0-8240-0597-X

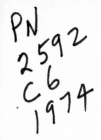
Contents

v

Preface

The closing of the theatres and suppression of playing in England, first nominally because of civil warfare in the land, was solemnized by an ordinance of both Lords and Commons in 1642. This was enacted on 2 September, and appeared in print as a last-page rider to the Declaration *of 3 September "appeasing . . . unlawful tumults and insurrections," itself first issued (Wing E 1411) without the terminal strictures on plays. We reprint the fuller state of the ordinance, Wing 1411 var., from a copy in the British Museum (E115[15.]); it collates A^4. Of this four-leaf edition a facsimile reprint was prepared c. 1820, without imprint (not in Lowe-Arnott-Robinson), and another by Joseph Knight in 1886 (Lowe-Arnott-Robinson 827); the full text is also given by Collier (1831) and by Hazlitt (1889, from Collier). Subsequent ordinances of 22 October 1647 and 11 February 1647/8 (Schelling,* Elizabethan Drama, *II, 370, erroneously dates this 1647) completed the suppression by reducing the legal status of all players to that of "rogues," within the meaning of the old Elizabethan and Jacobean statutes, and provided authority to officers for dismantling playhouses, called for the public whipping of practicing actors*

7

PREFACE

(at the first offense), confiscation of door-money, and fines of five shillings to be imposed on any spectator of an acted play. The three ordinances and evidence of their observation are discussed by Collier, Annals (1831), II, 104-119. We reprint the 1647 and 1648 decrees (Wing E 2413 and E 2070, Lowe-Arnott-Robinson 145 and 146) from copies in the British Museum (1130.c.7 and 517.k14[34]); each collates A^4. The former has been transcribed by Henry Scobell (1651), by Collier (1831), and by Hazlitt (1889), the latter by Scobell, Collier, Ashbee (facsimile, 1869), Charles Hindley (1873), and by Hazlitt.

In 1641, a year prior to the statutory closing of the theatres, plague had inhibited all theatrical performance from 5 August to 26 November. During this autumn appeared The Stage-Players Complaint, *an anonymous imaginary dialogue between the Fortune and Blackfriars actors Caine and Reed, who are immediately transformed in the text to "Quick" and "Light." There is not a great deal of theatrical matter contained in the satire, but it is certainly lively, above all with its reflections upon contemporary political attitudes toward the stage in the midnight hour of tolerance. Collier (Rarest Books, II, 381) knew of two copies only of the ill-printed squib; four are now recorded, of which we reprint the British Museum copy (E.172[23]), collating A^4. It is Wing S 5162, Lowe-Arnott-Robinson 141; there are transcripts*

PREFACE

of the text by Collier, Hazlitt, and Hindley, and a type-facsimile (1868) by E. W. Ashbee.

A few months after the inhibition of playing appeared (24 January 1643) The Actors Remonstrance, generally a sincere appeal on behalf of the theatrical fraternity for the restoration of their privileges, although larded with ironic solicitude for landladies, musicians, "hireling" players, and footloose gallants, all deprived of their proper activity by the closing of the theatres or by the financial straits of the former sharers. The spokesman-author piously claims an intensified morality both in the more recent theatrical environment (pickpockets and harlots banished, etc.) and in the scripts themselves, evidence enough that the tract had serious proselytic intent. Thomas Kenrick, E. W. Ashbee, Hindley, and Hazlitt republished The Actors Remonstrance; our reprint is from a copy in the British Museum (E86[8]), one of five known, collating A⁴. Wing A 453, Lowe-Arnott-Robinson 144.

The broadside petition to Parliament "of diverse poor and distressed men, heretofore the actors of Black-Friers and the Cock-Pit" [1650] is evidently not recorded by Wing, and known only from a specimen at Worcester College, Oxford. We reprint that copy, which has hitherto been edited with commentary by C. H. Wilkinson for the Luttrell Society (Theatre Miscellany, Oxford, 1953). It is apparently the only extant printed petition of its

PREFACE

sort (Lowe-Arnott-Robinson 151).

Finally, this volume contains a short earlier attack (1625) on the theatre by Alexander Leighton (?), and a much shorter bit of doggerel on the suppression of puppet-plays at Bartholomew Fair. The former, rather a pedestrian effort, may be the "treatise against stage-playes" mentioned by "Sion's Plea" Leighton, whose career is in effect one long exposure to persecution and punishment, in his Speculum Belli Sacri *(1624), but the attribution is not endorsed by* DNB *or* STC. *We reprint the British Museum copy (T1068[3]), collating A-C⁴ D² (Lowe-Arnott-Robinson 275; a transcript is given by Hazlitt).* The Dagonizing of Bartholomew Fayre *is reprinted from the unique broadside in the Thomason Collection of the British Museum (Wing D 109, Lowe-Arnott-Robinson 148). Wing does not record a reset edition of approximately the same date, omitting the ballad "I thanke you twice," extant at Harvard (Lowe-Arnott-Robinson 149); and there is a reprint of c. 1820 (Lowe-Arnott-Robinson 150) as well. The original text is reprinted by Hyder Rollins, "A Contribution to the History of the English Commonwealth Drama,"* Studies in Philology *XVIII (1921), 267-333, and its significance is discussed by George Speaight,* The History of the English Puppet Theatre *(1955).*

May, 1973   A. F.

10

A
SHORTE TREATISE
against
STAGE-PLAYES

Prov. 10. 23.
It is a ſport to a foole to doe miſchief.

Prov. 21. 17.
He that loues paſtime ſhall be a poore man.

Epheſ. 5. 11.
Haue no fellowſhip with the vnfruitfull works of darkneſſe, but rather reproue them.

Printed in the yeere of our Lord 1625.

AN HVMBLE
SVPPLICATION
TENDRED
to the High and Honourable Houſe
OF
PARLIAMENT,
Aſſembled May xviij.
1 6 2 5.

*Hereas Stage-playes are repugnant to
the written Word and Will of Al-
mightie God, the onely wiſe Gouernour
& righteous Judge of the whole world;
dangerous to the eternall ſaluation
both of the actours and ſpectatours ; breede many
inconueniences whereſoeuer they come ; procure the
judgments of God to the whole kingdome , for ſinne
tollerated pourchaſeth Gods wrath to the whole
nation, as appeareth Joſhu. 22. 18. and Sa-
lomon ſayth Prov. 14. 34. Sinne is a reproach to
my people ; and haue beene juſtly cenſured and*

worthily prohibited by Statutes made in the late Ragne of famouse Queene Elizabeth, and of our Learned and Noble King James: May it therefore please this High and Honourable House, which is the most honourable Court in all Europe, upon view of this short Treatise following, to take once more into consideration this matter of Stageplayes, and by some few words added to the former Statutes, to restreyne them for euer hereafter.

A SHORT TREATISE

OF

STAGE-PLAYES.

The Preface.

IN all ages the Prophets haue applied their preachings to the prefent occa-fions: and the generall concurffe of many baptifed Chriftians to Stage-playes, euery where in thefe times, haue occafioned the Lords remem-brancers, which ftand continually on their watch-towres, both more diligently to examine the na-ture of Stage-playes, which haue had much coun-tenance, and fome defenfe; to trie whether they be warrantable by the word of God or no; and alfo more earneft prayer to God for his affiftance, and ferious indeauours to diffwade Chriftians from en-tertayning them. Hence proceede thefe fewe en-fuing reafons, briefly contracted into a narrow roome, that the reader may with facilitie conceaue the force of the arguments, and foundly judge of

A 3   the

the trueth of them. And for better direction to the
Reader, the whole fumme is drawne to thefe foure
heads.

Firſt, the originall beginning of Stage-playes is
ſhewed : *ſect.* 2.

Secondly, the end is pointed out for which they
were firſt deviſed. *ſect.* 3.

Thirdly, the generall matter or argument acted in
them, is opened in few words : *ſect.* 4.

Fourthly, the reaſons to proue them vnlawfull are
rendred : *ſect.* 5.

I. *The originall beginning of Stage-playes.*

2. THe firſt beginning of playes proceeded
from thoſe men which were not in the
Church of God. When God had appoin-
ted man to get his liuing, with his labour Gen. 3.
19. Iuball the ſeauenth of Cain his race invented
playing. Gen.4.21.on Inſtruments, which (as after)
is a lawfull recreation. But the invention of divers
ſorts of vnlawfull playes is briefly noted by Plinius
Hiſtor. natur. lib. 7. cap. 59. by Euſebius de præ-
par. euang. lib. 1. cap. 2. and lib. 2. cap. 2. by Arnobius contra gentes lib. 7. by Polydorus Virgi-
lius de rerum invent. lib. 3. cap. 13. by Alexander
ab Alexandro genialium dierum. libr.6.cap.19. by
Cælius Rhodiginus antiq. lib. 8. cap. 7. Whether
they grew vp firſt at Lydia in Aſia as ſaith Herodotus lib.1. or at Athens in Græcia, as Polydorus Vir-
gilius lib. 3. cap.13. and Volaterranus lib.29. ca.11.
report, it is not materiall. Pauſanias in Eliacis writeth that Iphitus was admoniſhed by the oracle of
Apollo

Apollo to reftore the Olympike games. Iofephus
Scaliger poëtices lib. 1. cap. 22. &c. may fatiffie all
men that defire to reade more of this point. About
the beginning of the Perfian monarchie, which *The folemn beginning of*
was almoft 500 yeeres afore Chrift, and about the *playes.*
time of the Iewes returne out of the captivitie of
Babylon, this mifcreant author alwayes of fome
hurte, never of any good to Chriftian or heathen,
firft came abroade with great folemnitie, as it may
be gathered by Herodotus. Afterwards from thofe
Lydians in Afia, or from the Grecians at Athens,
came playes to Rome in the reigne of Tarquinius
Prifcus, as Eufebius noteth in his Chronologie at
the yeare of the world 4602. Hermanus Contra- *Alexander ab*
ctus at the yeare of the world 3341 noteth the *Alexand.*
fame. And Titus Livius lib.7. Pomponius Lætus *lib.5.c.16.*
in Philippo, Funccius in his worthie Chronologie
at the yeare of the world 3512. and Herodianus
lib. 3. witnes how the Romans augmented their
playes afterwards.

The firft authorifed entrance that any fuch kinde *The entrance*
of playes or heathen exercife had into the church *of playes into*
of God, feemeth to be about 170 yeares before the *the Church*
birth of Chrift, when that wicked Iefus affecting *of the Iewes.*
heathenifme, changed his name into Iafon, and for
150 talents of filver purchafed a commiffion of An-
tiochus Epiphanes king of Syria, that he might
erect a place for heathen exercifes at Ierufalem, and
traine up the youth of the Iewes in the cuftomes of
the Gentiles, 1 Maccab.1.12. Iofeph. antiq. lib. 12.
cap. 6. but more fpecially 2 Maccab. 4. 7. &c.
Which exercife though it was not to play on the
ftage, but for activitie of their bodies, yet it may
here

here be obſervèd as an entrance to other heathen
cuſtomes, and as that which maketh way to bring
in Stage-playes afterwards. Then Herode the
greate increaſed heatheniſh playes and exerciſes
greatly in his dayes, building one theater at Ieruſa-
lem; Ioſeph. antiq. lib. 15. cap. 10. or 11. and an
other at Cæſarea Stratonis; Ioſeph. antiq. lib. 15.
cap. 13. and lib. 16. cap. 9. The horrible ſinnes
of the Iewes cutte them off ſhortly after from being
the Church of God, and therefore no more can be
ſayd of their heatheniſh exerciſes.

Their en-
trance into
the chriſtia
church.
How or when Playes came into the Chriſtian
Church, and who firſt gaue them intertainment,
Is more incident to this preſent purpoſe, and fitter
teſtimonie to giue evidence hereafter either for
them or againſt them. When the Roman Emperours delighted too much in all kind of playes, and
when chriſtian religion grew mightily under them
in Europe eſpecially, chriſtians imbraceing the
Goſpel could not be altogether ignorant of theſe
ſtage-playes, but ſometimes ſome chriſtians reſor-
ted to theſe playes, as by the complaints and invec-
tiues of ſome ancient fathers againſt them, it doth
appeare. And though ſecretly by ſuch meanes playes
through ſatans ſubtilties approached neare to the
church doore, yet all this while neither the Emperours power thruſt them upon the Church, nor
the reverend Fathers and faithfull Paſtours of thoſe
times gaue way to ſuch open wickednes by theire
ſilence. But when that great ſcarlet coloured
whore of Babylon with her golden cup of abhomi-
nations in her hand, which hath a name written in
her forehead, a myſterie, great Babilon the mother

of whoredomes, and which reigneth over the
kings of the earth, was fet in Peters chaire at Rome
as the Papifts fay; then did the king of the Locufts,
called *Abaddon* and *Apollyon*, hauing the key of the
bottomeles pitt, with full power for fuch a purpofe, fette the church doore wide open for fundrie
fportes and playes to enter freely into the houfe of
God, as Platina reporteth Paulus II. did. And that
not onely in their great folemnities and feftivals,
which were fpent commonly in bellie cheare and
Playes, as Peucerus writeth of Vrbanus IIII. much
after the fafhion of the Ifraelites, fitting downe to
eate and drinke, and rifing up to play : but fpecially in their rich Iubilies, firft begunne in the Chriftian church by Bonifacius VIII. in the yeare of
Chrift 1300. and afterwards continued and haften-
ed by his fucceffors. Of which Sports and Playes
Aventinus annal. Bojor. lib. 7. fpeaking of Cle-
mens VI. and Bale in the life of Iulius III. doe
write. And thus much fhall fuffice for the beginning of Playes among the Lydians of Afia; and
among the Grecians and Romans in Europe; as alfo for their entrance into the Chriftian church, firft
fecretly by the malice of Satan ftealing fome Chriftians affedions to fuch vanities; then openly by
the power of that Abaddon of Rome, who befot-
ted mens fenfes with fuch fooleries, that he might
robbe their purfes in his rich Iubilies.

II. *The ende for which Playes were devifed.*

3. THe finall caufe or ende for which the Heathen firft devifed Playes, was to pacifie their
angrie

angrie gods, and so remoue some present calamitie which vexed them. The Lydians sought by Playes to remedie a greate famine that was among them, as Herodotus witnesseth in Clio. The Athenians renewed their Playes about the latter ende of the Persian Monarchie, in the dayes of Euthydemus their governour, thereby thinking to remoue a grievous pestilence, as sayth Diodorus Siculus lib. 12. Also Livius lib. 7. and Paulus Orosius libr. 3. cap. 4. write that the heathen Romans sore afflicted about the same time, with pestilence, by the advise of their idoll priests, set forth their Stage-playes to turne away that affliction, thinking their Playes would please their gods.

But Dionysius Halicarnasseus li. 7. Arnobius. lib. 7. contra gentes. Pausanias in Corinthiacis. Augustinus de civitate dei lib. 2. cap. 13. & lib. 3. cap. 18. & lib. 4. cap. 1. & cap. 26. Polydorus Virgil. de inventione rerum lib. 3. cap. 13. and Volaterranus lib. 29. cap. 11. write so plainly and fully of this matter, that the reading of any one of them may satisfie the sober minded, and giue them to understand, that as Christians by direction out of Gods word use prayer and fasting to turne away the Lords provoked anger: so heathens instructed by the Divell their master thought to remoue their afflictions by Playes. But the Popes of Rome solemnised their Festivals and Iubilies with all sortes of Playes and Sportes for recreation, and to delite the people with such fooleries.

III. The

III. *The argument of Stage-playes.*

4. WHereas Stage playes ordinarily goe under the name either of Tragedies or els
of comedies; we are to underſtand that
the argument or matter acted in tragedies is murther, treaſon, rebellion, and ſuch like; and in comedies is bauderie, coſenage, and meere kna-
verie.

But here ſome men eyther meerly ignorant (as *Objection.*
the moſt religious and learned are ignorant of ma-
ny things, *for we know but in part.* 1 Cor. 13. 9.) or *Bucerus de*
els perverſly irreligious, will ſay, that ſometimes *regno Chriſti*
the ſacred Scripture is or may be acted by players *lib. 2, ca. 54.*
on the ſtage, and thereby a man may learne more
then at a ſermon.

But for better information of the ignorant, and *Anſwer.*
more forcible confutation of the perverſe and profane, a threefold anſwer may be giuen.

Firſt, concerning thoſe perſons that ſo greatly *1. anſwer.*
deſire to learne religion at Stage-playes, let them
examine their owne conſciences by their workes
which are manifeſt before God and men, and con-
ſider themſelues in theſe fiue points.

1. They ſeldome come to the Church to learne
religion according to Gods ordinance, though
God command them ſo to doe, Deut. 12, 5. *But
ye ſhall ſeeke the place which the Lord your God ſhall chooſe
out of all your tribes, to put his name there, and there to
dwell, and thither thou ſhalt come,*&c. though God in-
treate them ſo to doe, Prov. 1. 20. *Wiſedome cryeth
without : ſhee uttereth her voyce in the ſtreets.* &c. as al-

ſo Prov. 9. 3. &c. and though they promiſed at their baptiſme ſo to doe.

2. They reade the Scriptures little or never at home, they catechiſe not their families, Deut 6, 7. or they are not catechiſed themſelues.

3. They haue little or no delite to conferre and talke of religion, but rather are wearie of ſuch as ſpeake to them of religion, avoide their companie, and call them Puritanes.

4. They leade not their life religiouſly, but follow the faſhion of the world eyther one way or other.

5. They reſort not to Stage-playes to learne religion, but to ſolace them ſelues in ſinne.

2. *anſwer.*   Secondly, concerning the Stage-players.

1. They are no greate Divines, no Doctors of divinitie, ſcarſe good profeſſors of religion.

2. They are not called of God to any ſuch publike function, as to be teachers of religion.

3. They are forbidden to meddle with religion Pſal. 50. 16. *What haſt thou to doe to declare mine ordinances that thou ſhouldeſt take my name in thy mouth; ſeeing thou hateſt to be reformed, and haſt caſt my wordes behinde thee?*

4. They abuſe ſcripture when they rehearſe it upon the ſtage, as conjurers and witches do in their inchantments, charmes, ſorceries, and conjurations.

5. They pollute Scripture when they mention it upon the Stage. For as the Prieſt anſwered Hag. 2. 14. that if a polluted perſon touched the ſacrifices, the oblation ſhould be uncleane: ſo if theſe

Stage-

Stage-players meddle with Scripture they pollute it.

Thirdly, concerning the Scripture it felfe. *3. anfwer.*

1. God ordeyned not that the Holy Scriptures fhould be acted upon the Stage, in fuch kinde of fcurrilitie, by fuch light and vaine perfons, nor to fuch ende as to make fporte and paftime; but with great reverence to be foberly handled, by faythfull and lawfull minifters, in the holy affemblies of the faintes.

2. The Scripture is Gods power to beate down finne, and not to mainteine it; to beget fayth, not to deftroy it; to bring men into Gods glorious kingdome, and not to throwe them downe into hell.

3. God fmote one Theopompus, an infidell, with Lunacie, for inferting Scripture in his writings, and one Theodoctes with blindnes for citing Scripture in his tragedie, as it is reported by Iofephus antiq. lib. 12. cap. 2. and by Eufebius de præparat. euangel. lib. 8. cap. 1.

Wherefore it is a profane thing to deale with Scripture upon the Stage, or in any fport and play, it is pernitious to the actors, hearers, and beholders.

IIII. *The reafons which proue Stageplayes to be unlawfull.*

The firft reafon.

5. **T**He firft reafon fhall be taken from their originall beginning, which was from the Heathen, *1 Reafon.*

B 5 then,

then, and to pacifie their idolls anger, that prefent afflictions might be removed, as hath been fhewed before; fect. 3. And therefore they feeme unlawfull for Chriftians, whom the Apoftle warneth to avoyd, not onely that which is evill, but alfo the very fhewe of evill. *Abfteyne from all appearance of evill.* 1 Theff. 5, 22. And in another place he fayth: *Furthermore, brethren, whatfoever things are true, whatfoever things are honeft, whatfoever things are juft, whatfoever things are pure, whatfoever things perteine to loue, whatfoever things are of good report, if there be any vertue, or if there be any prayfe, thinke on thefe things,* &c. Philip. 4, 8. Wherefore feeing there are none of thefe things in Stage-playes, and that they bring with them not onely appearance of evill, but evill it felfe, they may not be counted lawfull for Chriftians.

Objection.

But fome will fay, we haue no refpect to their heathenifh beginning or ufe, but now they ferue onely for recreation, and not otherwife.

Anfwer.

The anfwere firft fheweth what are lawfull recreations, and fecondly confuteth the objection.

Recreations.

Recreation is a meere compound Latine word, made Englifh by ufe, and fignifieth to *renew*, to *repaire*, to *recover*, to *reftore*, or to *refrefh* eyther the bodie, or the minde, or both, when they are impaired, overworne, wearied, or fpent in the imployments of mens lawfull callings, to the end that men recreated (for it feemeth convenient to reteyne the word) and refrefhed, may chearefully returne to their lawfull callings againe, and therein ferue God faythfully. Wherefore here are three things to be confidered.

Firft,

Firſt, that recreations are not alwayes neceſſarie, **1.**
nor to be permitted to all perſons, but onely to
thoſe that are overwearied with honeſt labour in
their lawfull callings.

Secondly, that recreations ſerue onely to refreſh **2.**
men, and make them fitter for the dueties of their
callings.

Thirdly, ſome recreations, which the Lord our **3.**
gratious God, and mercifull Father hath in his wiſedome and loue to his ſervants granted and thought
meete for the ſonnes of men, are particularly to be
mentioned, and namely theſe fiue ſpecially:

Firſt, ſome little reſt from labour, as if the reapers **1. Reſt.**
in harveſt.time may but ſit downe and reſt them
ſelues for one quarter of an houre, they will return
more freſhly to their worke againe. And ſo it is
with all other men, in what calling ſoever they are
occupied.

Secondly, foode meate and drinke, which re- **2. Foode.**
freſheth man comfortably, and maketh him fitter
and more able to performe the dueties of his calling.

Thirdly, ſleepe reneweth man and refreſheth him **3. Sleepe.**
greatly, that he is thereby, as if he had not beene
wearied before.

Fourthly, ſome change of labour quickeneth a **4. Change of labour.**
man, that his former wearines is forgotten.

Fiftly, Muſick is a chearefull recreation to the **5. Muſick.**
minde, that hath beene blunted with ſerious medi-
tations.

Theſe and ſuch like are holy and good recreations both comfortable and profitable, whereunto
may be added holy conference of good men concerning

cerning good and neceſſarie matters.

As for hawking, hunting, fiſhing, fouling, and ſuch like, they are rather to be counted honeſt and lawfull callings, wherein men may get their living with their labour, then recreations, except it be by change of labour, as in other lawfull callings.

Confutation. And now to come to confutation of the objection, it ſeemeth that Stage-playes cannot be counted in the number of recreations, and that for theſe three reaſons.

Firſt, they are not worhie to be compared to any of the former lawfull recreations.

Secondly, they ſerue not the ende of recreations, which is to refreſh the wearie, but not to make men delight in ſinne.

Thirdly, the moſt perſons that ordinarily reſorte to them, are verie idle perſons, that ſhould rather be ſet to ſome honeſt labour, then ſo unprofitably to miſpend their time to their owne hurte.

The originall beginning then is ſufficient to perſwade the faythfull to renounce Stage-playes, and ſay unto them, *Gette thee hence.* Eſai. 30. 22.

The ſecond reaſon.

2 Reaſon. 6. THE ſecond reaſon may be taken from the matter or argument, which is acted upon the Stage, which is eyther murther and miſchief in tragedies, or bauderie and coſonage in comedies, as was obſerved before ſect. 4. And the reaſon may be contrived thus.

It is not lawfull for Chriſtians to ſporte themſelues eyther with the dreadfull judgments of
God

God, or with the abhominable finnes of men.

But in Stage-playes there are acted fometimes the fearefull judgments of God, as in tragedies: andfometimes the vile and hatefull finnes of men, as in comedies.

And therefore it is full of horrour ferioufly to thinke upon them, and much more to be eyther actor to fhew them, or beholder and hearer to laugh at them, or delite in them.

Ham derided his Fathers nakednes Gen. 9, 22. but he was accurfed for it. Curfes are denounced in Gods Law againft all finners, Deut. 27, 26. And they that make a fport of finne cannot avoyd Gods curfe, no more then they that feafted when they fhould haue fafted, Efay. 22, 14. *Surely this iniquitie fhall not be purged from you, till ye dye, fayth the Lord of Hoaftes.*

The third reafon.

7. **T**HE third reafon is taken from the Stage-players, and from fuch their vices as properly belong to them, as they are Stage-players. And four of their vices may perfwade all men that their playes are unlawfull. ; Reafon.

Firft, they being men, change their apparel, and put on womans apparell, without which exchange they cannot act fome partes in their Playes, which thing the Lord forbiddeth. Deut. 22. 5. *The woman fhall not weare that which perteyneth to the man, neyther fhall a man put on womans rayment: for all that do fo are an abomination to the Lord thy God.* For this change of apparell maketh the man effeminate, and the

                                  I.

C   woman

woman maniſh, as ſome can teſtifie if they would,
ſome haue confeſſed, and the Heathen know. Cyprianus lib. 2. epiſt. 2. ſpeaking of this change of
apparell in Stage-playes, ſayth thus : *euirantur ma-*
res ; men looſe their manhood &c.   Charondas
made a law to the inhabitants of Thuria (which is a
citie in Greece , deſcribed by Pauſanias in Meſſeni-
cis, and by Strabo lib. 8.) that if any man refuſed
to goe to warres, or being in the field caſt downe
his weapons and ranne away , he ſhould ſtand three
dayes in the open market in womans apparell,
which argued effeminatenes in him , as if formerly
he had uſed it. Diodor. lib. 12.

2.   Secondly , they never come on the Stage in
theire owne name, but ſome in the name and perſon of a divell, others of a foole, others of a bawde,
others of a tyrant, others of other men, which be-
ſeemeth not a Chriſtian, neither proceedeth it of
God, nor is approved of God, but is contrarie to
Chriſtian profeſſion. Tit. 2. 12.

3.   Thirdly , they ſweare vainly by the living God,
which is contrarie to the Law of God , Exod. 20. 7.
or by heathen idols, which is forbidden , Exod.
23. 13. or by both, which is reproved Amos 8. 14.
Zephan. 1. 5.

4.   Fourthly, they teach their hearers and beholders
much ſinne in the acting of their Playes ; as to
ſweare, curſe, lye, flatter, coſen, ſteale, to play
the bawde and the harlot, with very many ſuch
other lewde leſſons.

The fourth Reason.

8. **T**HE fourth reason ariseth from the consi- ~ 4 Reason.
deration of the hearers and beholders,
who being baptised into the name of
Christ, are brought into danger of gods wrath, and
their owne condemnation, in as much as they are
partakers of the sinnes of the Players and of the
Playes in approving them. And whatsoever brings
men into these dangers must needs be evill. And
besides the approbation, which maketh them guil-
tie, they learne sinne: for as sayth Cyprianus lib.
2. epist. 2. *adulterium discitur, dum videtur,* they
learne to commit adulterie, when they heare and
behold such immodest and unchaste words and ge-
stures upon the stage. And many goe honest thither, which returne home dishonest. Iob made a
covenant with his eyes, that he would not looke
on a maide, Iob 31. 1. David desired God to turne
away his eyes from regarding vanitie, Psal. 119. 37.

The fift Reason.

9. **T**HE fift reason may be taken from con- ~ 5 Reason.
sideration of these eight fruits or effects
which follow Stage-playes:
First, the Stage-players get their living by an un-   1.
godly & unlawfull trade, never approved by God,
& when they shall stand at the barre of Gods judgement, they shall be speachles; and cast into utter
darkenes, where shall be weeping and gnashing of
teeth, except they repent and forsake their wicked

trade betimes, whiles the Lord granteth fpace to repentance.

2.   Secondly, the hearers receaue much hurte by them, as was noted in the fourth reafon, and if it be true which is reported, whoredome is fometimes committed at that place, and at that time.

3.   Thirdly, the better fort of men which are governours of families, receaue domage, when fome of their families reforte to Stage-playes, for fometimes their goods are ftollen to mainteine Lewdnes, fometimes their daughters or maide-fervants are defiled, or ftollen away, and maried without their governours confent or privitie.

4.   Fourthly, the word of God and the minifters thereof, are now and then taxed and taunted.

5.   Fiftly, the Lord himfelfe is there blafpheamed ordinarily.

6.   Sixtly, the poore in the church of Chrift, are
dii.86, c.8 hindred from fome reliefe, which otherwife they might haue. for the prodigalitie lavifhed upon Stage-players, reftrayneth the liberalitie that might and ought to be beftowed upon the poore.

7.   Seauenthly, there is loffe of pretious time, which fhould be fpent in Gods fervice, by thofe that are hired to be diligent labourers in his vineyard, and not be wickedly mifpent in fuch finfull fportes, feeing everie one, both young and olde, muft giue account to God of his labours, and of his time fpent in this life. The Holy Ghoft fayth Ephef. 5. 16. *Redeeme the time, for the dayes are evill*; but fome men fay, Let us haue paftime, that is, any finfull courfe, whereby we may paffe away & mif-fpend the fhort time which we haue in this life, that the day of

death,

death, judgment, and condemnation may come speedily upon us before we repent, and before we confecrate our felues wholly to God. Peter fayth: *It is fufficient for us, that we haue fpent the time paft of this life, after the luftes of the Gentiles, walking in wantonnes, luftes, drunkennes, in gluttonie, drinkings, and abominable idolatries.* 1 Pet. 4. 3. And if any be otherwife minded, the Lord in his time will either convert or confound him.

Eightly, whereas the life of a Chriftian effectually called, fhould be fpent continually in fighting againft all kinde of finne, in crucifying the old man, and in renewing the inner man dayly, thefe Stageplayes quench the fpirit, and deftroy the new man, as alfo on the other part, they fofter, cherifh, and mainteyne the old man, as all thofe that haue the fpirit of Chrift know and feele. But *if any man haue not the fpirit of Chrift, the fame is not his.* Rom. 8. 9.

8.

The fixth Reafon.

10. THE fixt reafon may be taken from the opinion and judgment of all fortes and ftates of men, by whom thefe Stageplayes haue been difalowed.

6 Reafon.

Firft, all orthodoxall Proteftants of all ages and times, which maintayned the generall doctrine of the Catholike church, haue cenfured Stage-playes, as unlawfull from age to age hitherto. To reporte and repeate their feverall judgements out of their owne writings, or out of hiftories, is more then I can performe, it would make a great volume, it

1, Orthodoxal Proteftants.

would

would be tedious to reade, and perhaps not so ne-
ceffarie.

Wherefore it feemeth rather convenient to call
a greate number of them together out of all the places of their dwellings, and as it were out of all the
world, that they all may be heard to fpeake altogether with one confent and voyce. But becaufe it
would be a verie tedious, and troublefome thing,
for fo many, fo reverend, and fo old aged Fathers
to travell fo farre ; it is more convenient and reafo-
nable to fpare their labours fo much as may be, and
call them together at three feverall times, and in
three feverall places of their habitations; that is, to
call thofe of Afia, to meete together in Afia : thofe
of Africa, in Africa: and thofe of Europe, in
Europe.

Afia,   In Afia, about two and twentie of the moft reverend Fathers of thofe times, met together in Laodicea, fomewhat more then 300 yeres after Chrift,
and holding a councill there, decreed cap. 54. that
none of the Cleargie fhould be prefent at Stage-
playes. And the Centuriators of Magdeburg haue
inferted this whole Councill in their laborious and
worthie hiftorie Cent. 4. cap. 9. col. 834.

Afrike.   In Africa more then 400 years after Chrift there
were fome four and fortie of the worthieft & lear-
nedft Fathers affembled at Carthage in the third
councill that was holden there, amongft whom
was that worthie Auguftinus, and they decreed
cap. 11. that the children of minifters or of others
of the Cleargie fhould not be prefent at Stage-
playes, feeing none of the Laitie might be there.
Semper enim Chriftianis omnibus hoc interdictum eft, ut
ubi

ubi blasphemi sunt, non accedant. that is ; for all christians haue evermore beene forbidden to come in
place, where blasphemers are. And the same religious Fathers then, and there decreed also cap. 35.
That the church should not tesuse to receaue the
Stage-players into their fellowship, if they repen-
ted and renounced that their trade of playing.
Whereby is evident thatStage-players in those former and purer times, were generally excommuni-
cated, and cast out of the societie of the saintes.

In Europe divers worthie and graue Fathers of Europe.
the church, called and summoned by Constantinus.
Magnus, a little after the Nicene Councill, to come
together at Arles in France, held two Councils there,
the first, and shortly after the second. In both which
they decreed the excommunication of all Stage-
players, so long as they continued that trade of
life. And in the first Councill, cap. 5. thus they
say : *De theatricis, & ipsos placuit, quandiu agunt, à
communione separari* ; that is, as touching Stage-
players, we thinke it good, that whiles they continue in that trade of life, they be kept from the com-
munion. And in the second Councill held there
presently after, they decree the same thing againe,
can. 20. and almost in the same words.

But yet to giue in more evidence, we may haue
all the worthie Fathers of the Churches in Asia,
Africa, and Europa, assembled together in the sixt
generall Council, which was held at Constanti-
nople, approue that which at Laodicea in Asia, and
at Carthage in Africa, was decreed against Stage-
players. For when Constantinus Pogonatus in the
yeare 681 called that sixt general Councel at Con-
stantinople

ftantinople againft the Monothelites of thofe times, as Zonoras, Tomo tertio fheweth, about fiue yeares after, his fonne Iuftinianus II. affembled the Fathers there againe, as Gratianus dift. 16. cap. 7. and the Centuriators of Magdeburgh, Cent. 7. cap. 9. col. 455. doe witneffe : and can. 20. they approue thofe two former Councils of Laodicea and of Carthage.

And thus we haue the judgement of all the orthodoxall and true Catholike Fathers of the churches throughout the whole world, againft Stageplayers, and Stage-playing, with one confent.

2, Papifts. Secondly, the Papifts, though they be fauourers of Stage-playes, and actors fometime upon the Stage (as lately at Lions in France) yet they cannot for verie fhame juftifie them, but contrariewife condemne them in their writings. And in their great Canon booke of Decrees compiled by Gratian, they ratifie the four firft generall Councils, and all the other Councils made afterwards, and conteyned in that greate booke of Decrees, dift. 15. cap. 2. & 4. and dift. 16. cap. 6. &c. they approue by name the three Councils alledged before. More particularly they approue that which was mentioned before of the Council of Laodicea, de confecratione dift. 5. cap. 37. and that which was decreed againft Stage-plaies in the third Councill of Carthage, de confecrat. dift. 2. cap. 96. and the canons of the fixt generall Councill, de confecratione dift. 3. cap. 29.

3, Parlement. Thirdly, the Honourable Court of Parliament in this Land, hath juftly cenfured Stage-players, as thofe that liue not in a lawfull trade to mainteyne
them-

themfelues by. as in the xiiij. yeare of Elizabeth,
chap. 5. and in the xxxix yeare of Elizab. chap. 7.
and in the fecond yeare of King *Iames*, chap. vij.

Fourthly, the civill law in pointing out thofe
perfons which are of evill note or name, fayth thus
of Stage-players Pandect. lib. 3. tit. 2. *Eos enim, qui
quæſtus cauſa in certamina deſcendunt, & omnes propter
præmium in ſcenam prodeuntes, famoſos eſſe, Pegaſus &
Nerva reſponderunt;* that is, Pegafus and Nerva faid,
that thofe were infamous which tryed maſterie for
gaine, and all that came upon the Stage for a re-
warde.　Alfo who lift, may reade fomewhat to the
fame purpofe. Novel. conft. 51.

*4, The civill
Law.*

Fiftly, the infidell Heathens, howfoever they
firft devifed them, and after ufed them very much,
yet haue they difalowed them, as Auguftine de civitate Dei, lib. 2. cap. 13. rehearfing the words of
Scipio out of Tullie, fheweth : *Quum artem ludi-
cram ſcenamque totam probro ducerent, genus id homi-
num non modo honore civium reliquorum carere, ſed etiam
tribu moveri notatione cenſoria voluerunt.* that is, The
Romans accounting thofe playes, and the whole
Stage to be reproachfull, when they valued the
goods and enrolled the names of their citizens,
gaue not the honour of other citizens to Stage-
players, but razed their names out of their wardes
or companies. Suetonius taxeth Nero for a favo-
rer of them, and an actor among them. Arnobius
lib. 7. contra gentes, appealing to the confcience
of the Heathen, fheweth that they difallow them,
and fayth thus of the Stage-players, *actores inhoneſtos
eſſe jus veſtrum judicavit,* that is, your owne law hath
adjudged the ftage-players to be no honeft men.

5, Heathens.

And thefe judgements of men are fufficient to
condemne Stage-playes as unlawfull, and difhoneft
alfo, as Cornelius Nepos fayth in his preface before
the defcription of the noble Emperours.

7 Reafon. 11. THE feauenth and laft reafon is drawne
from the judgments which God hath
inflicted upon the Players, and beholders.

1. Philip king of Macedonia, and father of Alexander the greate, was flaine at a play by Paufanias,
as Diodorus Siculus writeth lib. 16.

Plinius hiftor. natur. lib. 7. cap. 53. fpeaking of
divers that dyed fodainly, fayth, that one M. Ofi-
lius Hilarus a noble player of Comedies, after he
had played his part gallantly on the day of his birth,
and was vaunting at fupper of his dayes worke, died
fodainly at the table.

3. Paulus Orofius lib. 7. cap. 4. writeth that in
the twelft yeare of Tiberius, (which was three
yeares before Chrift beganne to preach the Gofpel
publikely) there were twentie thoufand perfons
flaine by the fall of the Theater at Fidena in Italie.

4. About thirteene yeares after, Caius Caligula
the Emperour was flaine at a play. Iofeph.antiq.lib.
19. cap. 1. Suetonius in Caligula cap. 58.

5. About 150 yeares after Chrifts nativitie,
whiles the Playes were kept at Rome with great
folemnitie, for the fpace of three dayes and three
nights together, continually and without inter-
miffion,

miſſion, a great parte of the citie was ſette on fire and conſumed. And Phillip the Emperour was ſlayne at Varona, and his ſonne at Rome, as it is reported by Sextus Aurelius, Pomponius Lætus, and Eutropius lib. 9.

6. Tertullianus in his booke de Spectaculis, ſayth, that a Chriſtian woman going to the playes, was then poſſeſſed of a divell, and when other Chriſtians, intending to caſt the divell out of her, demanded of him, how he durſt pre-ſume to aſſault one that beleeved in Chriſt, the divell anſwered, that he found her in his owne houſe, and therefore had good right to ſeaze upon her. Alſo he writeth in the ſame Booke and place, that an other faythfull woman going alſo to behold the Playes, had eyther a feare-full dreame or a viſion the next night after, wherein ſhee was checked for going to the Playes, was warned of her death, and dyed within fiue dayes after.

7. Aventinus annal. Bojorum lib. 7. writeth, that about 1200 yeares after Chriſt, three hun-dred men were ſlaine with hayle and lightning at Piſonium, a cittie of Bavaria, in the confines of Italie, whiles they were there to behold the Playes.

8. The ſame Author Aventinus annal. Bojor. lib. 7. writeth alſo, that when Pope Nicholaus V. ſolemnized his rich Iubilie, in the yeare 1450, with Stage-playes, fiue hundred & threeſcore per-ſons, comming to Rome to behold the Playes, were partly troden to death, and partly drowned in Tiber.

9. At

9. At London in the yeare of Chriſt 1583 eight perſons were ſlaine, and more hurte , by the fall of the theater.

10. At Lions in France in the moneth of Auguſt, in the yeare 1607 , whiles the Ieſuites were acting their Playes , to the diſgrace of true religion , and the profeſſors thereof, the Lord from heauen con‑ tinuing thunder & lightnings , for the ſpace of two houres together , ſlewe twelue perſons pre‑ ſently, and amaſed all the reſt with great terrour and feare.

F I N I S.

THE
STAGE-PLAYERS
COMPLAINT.

IN

A pleasant Dialogue betweene CANE of
the *Fortune*, and REED of the *Friers*.

Deploring their sad and solitary conditions for
want of Imployment.

In this heavie and Contagious time of the Plague
in LONDON.

LONDON,
Printed for THO: BATES, and are to be sold at his shop in the
Old-Bailey. 1641.

The Stage-Players complaint.

Cane.

STay *Reed*? Whither away so speedily? What
you goe, as if you meant to leape over the Moon
now ? What's the matter ?

Reede. The matter is plain enough : You incuse me
of my nimble feet; but I thinke your tongue runnes a
little faster, and you contend as much to out-strip fa-
cetious *Mercury* in your tongue, as lame *Vulcan* in
my feete.

Quick. Me thinks you're very eloquent: Prithee tell
me, Don't *Suada*, and the Jove-begotten-braine *Miner-*
va lodge in your facundious tongue : You have without doubt some great cause of alacrity, that you produce such eloquent speeches now. Prithee what is't ?

Light. How? Cause of alacrity? S'foot I had never
more cause of sorrow in my life : And dost thou tell
me of that ? Fie, fie !

Quick. Prithee why ? I did but conjecture out of
your sweet words.

Light. Well ! I see you'le never be hanged for a
Conjurer. Is this a world to be merry in ? Is this an
age to rejoyce in ? Where one may as soone find honesty in a Lawyers house, as the least cause of mirth in
the world. Nea you know this well enough, but onely you love to be inquisitive, and to search the Na-
ture of men.

Quick.

Quick. You fay true indeed : J cann't deny but that
the world doe fwell with griefe-bedaubing cares. For
illuftrate the whole Univerfe, from *Aurora's* purple
doores, to the Occidentall Weft, and you fhall finde
all things drowned in the floods of forrow. And no
marvaile too : For here Gods heavy hand doth punifh,
there man's oppreffion doe raigne : And what greater
affliction can be expected, then that both of God and
Man.

Light. 'Tis true : And now a dayes tis very diffi-
cult to live without one of them.

Quick. Revolve all humane nature : Here you may
fee a man pufft up with the winde of popular ap-
plaufe, climing to the top of Honour, but being once
touch't with the breath of Iuftice, oh in what a mo-
ment doth he tumble downe. There you may fee one
oppreffed with the tyranny of difgrace, and groaning
vnder the burden of calamity, but being fmil'd upon
by Juftice, oh how fuddainly is he mounted up with
the wings of Fame. There you may perceive women
lamenting the deaths of their poore Husbands ; here
one deploring the Churches Anarchie: there one grie-
ving at Fortunes malignity : fo that in the whole
world fuch diverfe ftreames of forrow doe flow every
where : that if they fhould meet : they would eafily
make up an Ocean.

Light. You fpeake of the Epidemicall caufe, that
produceth univerfall griefe, but you fhall not need,
for we our felves have caufe enough to mourne for
our owne mif-fortune, and not to participate with
the griefe of the whole world.

Well ! wee muſt ſubmit our ſelves to Gods all-diſpoſing providence, who in his owne time will give a period to our irregular teares. But our cauſe of ſorrow, is the cauſe of the whole world : For i'me perſwaded that there's never a *what lack you Sir* in all the City, but is ſenſible of our calamity too, although we ſeeme to them to beare the greateſt burthen thereof,

Light. I beleeve thee : therefore I thinke, they may well commiſſerate our cauſe with their own, and not account us ſo ridiculous to the vulgar ſpectacle of the world. For when we rejoyce, they doe all rejoyce with us ; but when wee lament, they have all cauſe to lament too : wherefore let not that thing trouble you ſo much.

Quick. Ay, come, let us omit this patheticall paſ-ſion, and thinke on the brave times which wee have had heretofore : Oh, the times, when wee have va-poured in the ſtreets like Courtiers.

Light. A pritty compariſon ! like Courtiers in-deed ; for I thinke our pockets were as empty as the proudeſt of them.

Quick. Oh the times, when my tongue have ranne as faſt upon the Scæane, as a *Windebankes* pen over the Ocean.

Light. Oh the times, when my heeles have ca-poured over the Stage as light as a *Finches* Fea-ther.

Quick. But (alas) we muſt looke for no more of theſe times I feare.

Light.

Light. Why fo ? Doft thou thinke becaufe a cloud fometimes may cover and obnubilate the Sun, that it will therefore fhine no more ? Yes I'le warrant you, and that more bright too : fo never feare Boy, but we fhall get the day agen for all this.

Quick. But i le affure you 'tis to be feared : For Monopolers are downe, Projectors are downe, the High Commiffion Court is downe, the Starre-chamber is down, & (fome think) Bifhops will downe : and why fhould we then that are farre inferior to any of thofe not juftly feare leaft we fhould be downe too ?

Light. Pifh, I can fhow thee many infallible reafons to the contrary : we are very neceffary and commodious to all people : Firft for ftrangers, who can defire no better recreation, then to come and fee a Play : then for Citizens, to feaft their wits: then for Gallants, who otherwife perhaps would fpend their money in drunkenneffe, and lafcivioufneffe doe find a great delight and delectation to fee a Play : then for the learned, it does increafe and adde wit, conftructively to wit: then for Gentlewomen, it teacheth them how to deceive idleneffe : then for the ignorant, it doe's augment their knowledge, Pifh, a thoufand more Arguments I could adde, but that I fhould weary your patience too much : Well! in a word we are fo needfull for the Common good, that in fome refpect it were almoft a finne to put us downe : therefore let not thefe frivolous things perplex your vexatious thoughts.

Quick. But it makes me feare i'le affure you in thefe times : And I thinke it would be a very good plot to borrow good ftore of money and then runne away : what thinke you of it ?

Light.

Light. A good plot, quother? So you may come to lie in a worser plot for it all the dayes of your life. S'foot runne away too? So you may be taken for a young *Suckling*, and then followed presently with a hundred Horse. Fie, fie, remit these fopperies, you little thinke of the laſt Comedy you acted now.

Quick. The laſt Comedy quother? I act Tragedies every day, but I cannot remember ſince I acted a Comedy, 'tis ſo long agoe.

Light. But Prithee how comes it to paſſe that you act Tragedies every day.

Quick. How? J'le tell thee: my purſe each day periſheth moſt Tragædically: and now J may be taken for a Scholler, ſince J've no money, but becauſe I cannot ſpeake true Latine, I'me afraid, I ſhall be taken for a Lawyer.

Light. What do's Lawyers then ſpeake falſe Latin?

Quick. As if you know not that! Why? True Latine is as much out of faſhion at *Innes of Court*, as good cloathes at *Cambridge*.

Light. Come, come remit your jeſts, and thinke on our preſent eſtates now: and you know the Sickneſſe is dangerous, and increaſeth weekly; therefore I think we muſt be content in the meane while to live like *Diogenes* in his Tub.

Quick. Well! the beſt remedy that J can imagine for our preſent Calamitie, is to downe on our knees humbly, and pray God to abate the Sickneſſe, and let each true hearted Subject conjoyne with us in our ſupplication.

Light. This motion pleaſeth mee exceedingly, come let us goe to ſome other friends, and unitely joyne in our Prayers.   *Quick*.

Quick. A match, come let us performe it with expedition : and in the meane while let us conclude with part of our Letany.

From Plague, Pestilence, and Famine, from Battell, Murder, and suddaine Death :

Good Lord deliver us.

FINIS,

A DECLARATION

Of The
LORDS and COMMONS
Assembled in *Parliament*,

For the appeasing and quietting of
all unlawfull Tumults and Insurrections in
the severall Counties of England, and
Dominion of Wales.

Die *Veneris*, Septemb. 2. 1642.

Ordered by the Lords and Commons Assembled in Par-
liament, that this Declaration shall be forthwith Printed, and
afterwards published in all Market Townes, Parish·Chur-
ches, and Chappels, within the Kingdome of England, and
Dominion of Wales, *and especially in the County·of* Essex.
Iohn Browne Cler. Parliament.

Also an Ordinance of both Houses,
for the suppressing of *Stage-Playes*.

Ordered by the Lords and Commons, that this Order be forth-
with Printed and Published.

Iohn Browne Cler. Parliament.

Septemb. 3. London Printed for *Iohn Wright*. 1642.

Die Veneris 2 Septem. 1642.

A Declaration of the L O R D S and Commons aſſembled in PARLIAMENT.

The Lords and Commons having lately ſent Sir *Thomas Barrington*, aud M. *Grymſtone*, into the County of *Eſſex*, for the appeaſing and quieting of divers Aſſemblies of peoole gathered together in a great bodies, who had much damnified the houſes, and taken the goods of divers perſons without Law or other authority; And having received a report from Sir *Thomas Barringion* being returned,

A 2   that

that the people upon the first knowledge given them
that the Parliament required they should forbear the
searching of any houses for Armes and Ammuni-
tion, or the taking goods out of any House other-
wise then is or shall be directed by the Parliament,
or without the assistance of some of those persons
who are by both Houses of Parliament declared
that they ought to be present; The people did
thereupon presently yeeld obedience and with-
drew themselves in a peaceable manner, and as they
were required, did make restitution of Plate, Money, and many other goods by them taken from
such as were pretended popish Recusants, and o-
ther malignant persons, and that they had expressed great zeale and forwardnesse to comply with
the directions of Parliament for the future. The
Lords and Commons doe declare, that they re-
scent the aforesaid expressions of the people, and
their ready obedience, as a testimony of that duti-
full affection which they beare to the Parliament,
and to the present service of the Kingdome, & doe
hereby order and declare, that all persons whosoever, that have taken either Mony, Plate or any other
Goods out of the House or Houses, or from the
persons of any whosoever, without the speciall
commaud or Order of both, or either House of
Parliament, shall forthwith restore the same to the
parties, from whome they were taken, or other-
wise be proceeded against, as the Lords and Commons shall furtherdirect, upon complaiut made,

And

And as both *Houses* of Parliament have beene, and will be very carefull to preserve the peace of the Kingdome, by disarming of all Recusants, and such others as shall be knowne or justly suspected to be enemies thereunto, and to the pious and good endeavours of this Parliament; And to that purpose have by a Declaration passed by assent of both Houses, the three and twentieth of *August* last, expressed what persons shall be intrusted for the managing of that service; They doe thereby further Order and Command, that no person doe presume either alone, or accompanied with others, to break or violently enter the House of any whosoever, under colour of pretence of disarming Recusants or other persons pretended to be enemies to the peace of the Kingdome; without the particular command of such as are intrusted or deputed by the Parliament; And it is further declared, that speciall and speedy care be taken therein, for the security of the Kingdome; and particularly for the County of *Essex*, from whom they have received so many expressions of their duty to the service of the publike, though the Parliament cannot but let them know, that severall violent actions by some of them unwarrantably committed, are extreamly disallowed; but as the Lords and Commons declare, that they shall be ever ready to give assistance, and protection to all such as shall obey the commands of both, or either Houses of Parliament, so they doe resolve, that they will inflict exemplary pu-

nishment

nifhment on all such according to their severall demerits, as shall be refractory and disobedient to these their commands made knowne to them; and by all good wayes, and meanes will further endeavour to bring them to a legall tryall for such their Offences; But for the incouragement of those who have beene forward, and active in the service of the Common-wealth, It is thought fit to give them notice, that those eight Horses taken from Sir *John Lucas*, and brought up to the Parliament by Sir *Thomas Barrington*, and intended by Sir *John Lucas*, for the strengthning of a Malignant party, and are delivered by command to the Lord Generall to be by him imployed for the preservation of the Kingdome, and the Parliament hath caused the same Sir *John Lucas*, and M. *Newcomen*, to bee committed to severall prisons; And it is Resolved, that they shall be brought to their severalls tryalls and receive such punishment as shall appeare to be just according to their demerits. And like proceedings shall be had against all such as shall bee found disturbers of the peace of that County.

WHereas the diftreffed E-
ftate of Ireland, fteeped
in her own Blood, and the diftra-
cted Eftate of England, threatned
with a Cloud of Blood, by a Civill Warre, call for all poffible
meanes to appeafe and avert the
Wrath of God appearing in thefe
Judgements; amongft which, Fa-
fting and Prayer having bin often
tryed to be very effectuall, have
bin lately, and are ftill enjoyned;
and whereas publike Sports doe
not well agree with publike
Calamities, nor publike Stage-
playes with the Seafons of Humiliation, this being an Exercife
of fad and pious folemnity, and
the other being Spectacles of
pleafure

pleasure, too commonly expres-
sing laciuious Mirth and Levitie:
It is therefore thought fit, and Or-
deined by the Lords and Commons in this Parliament, Assembled, that while these sad Causes
and set times of Humiliation doe
continue, publike Stage-playes
shall cease, and bee forborne. In-
stead of which, are recommended
to the people of this Land, the
profitable and seasonable Consi-
derations of Repentance, Recon-
ciliation, and peace with God,
which probably may produce
outward peace and prosperity, and
bring againe Times of Joy and
Gladnesse to these Nations.

Die Veneris, Septemb. 2. 1 6 4 2.
Ordered by the Lords and Commons in Parliament,
that this Order be forthwith Printed and published..
John Browne Cler. Parl.

FINIS.

THE
ACTORS
REMONSTRANCE,
OR
COMPLAINT:
FOR
The filencing of their profeffion, and banifhment from their feverall *Play-houfes*.

In which is fully fet downe their grievan-
ces, for their reftraint; efpecially fince Stage-
playes, only of all publike recreations are prohibited ; the exercife at the Beares
Colledge, and the motions of Pup-
pets being ftill in force
and vigour.

As it was prefented in the names and behalfes of
all our London Comedians to the great God P ĦŒ B U S-
A P O L L O, and the nine Heliconian Sifters, on the top of
P E R N A S S U S, by one of the Mafters of Re-
quefts to the M U S B S, for this
prefent month.

And publifhed by their command in print by the Typo-
graph Royall of the Caftalian Province. 1643.

LONDON, Printed for EDW. NICKSON.
Iannar. 24. 1643.

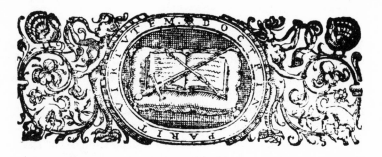

The *Actors* Remonstrance or Com-
plaint, for the filencing of their *Profeßion*,
and banifhment from their feverall
PLAY-HOUSES.

Ppreffed with many calamities, and
languifhing to death under the bur-
then of a long and (for ought wee
know) an everlafting reftraint, we
the *Comedians*, *Tragedians* and
Actors of all forts and fizes be-
longing to the famous private and
publike Houfes within the City of
London and the Suburbs thereof, to
you great *Phœbus*, and you facred Sifters, the fole Patroneffes
of our diftreffed Calling, doe we in all humility prefent this
our humble and lamentable complaint, by whofe intercef-
fion to thofe powers who confined us to filence, wee hope
to be reftored to our priftine honour and imployment.

Firft, it is not unknowne to all the audience that have
frequented the private Houfes of *Black-Friers*, the Cock-Pit
and *Salisbury-Court*, without aufterity, wee have purged our
Stages from all obfcene and fcurrilous jefts; fuch as might
either be guilty of corrupting the manners, or defaming the
perfons of any men of note in the City or Kingdome; that
A 2   wee

wee have endevoured, as much as in us lies, to inftruct one another in the true and genuine Art of acting, to repreffe bawling and railing, formerly in great requeft, and for to fuite our language and action to the more gentile and naturall garbe of the times; that we have left off for our owne parts, and fo have commanded our fervants, to forget that ancient cuftome, which formerly rendred men of our quality infamous, namely, the inveigling in young Gentlemen, Merchants Factors, and Prentizes to fpend their patrimonies and Mafters eftates upon us and our Harlots in Tavernes; we have cleane and quite given over the borrowing money at firft fight of punie gallants, or praifing their fwords, belts and beavers, fo to invite them to beftow them upon us; and to our praife be it fpoken, we were for the moft part very well reformed, few of us keeping. or being rather kept by our Miftreffes, betooke our felves wholy to our wives; obferving the matrimoniall vow of chaftity, yet for all thefe conformities and reformations, wee were by authority (to which wee in all humility fubmit) reftrained from the practice of our Profeffion; that Profeffion which had before maintained us in comely and convenient Equipage; fome of us by it meerely being inabled to keepe Horfes (though not Whores) is now condemned to a perpetuall, at leaft a very long temporary filence, and wee left to live upon our fhifts, or the expence of our former gettings, to the great impoverifhment and utter undoing of our felves, wives, children, and dependants; befides which, is of all other our extremeft grievance, that Playes being put downe under the name of publike recreations; other publike recreations of farre more harmfull confequence permitted, ftill to ftand *in ftatu quo prius*, namely, that Nurfe of barbarifme and beaftlineffe, the *Beare-Garden*, whereupon their ufuall dayes, thofe Demy-Monfters, are baited by bandogs, the Gentlemen of *Stave* and *Taile*, namely, boyftrous Butchers, cutting Coblers, hard-handed Mafons, and the like, rioting companions, reforting thither with as much freedome as formerly, ma-

king

king with their sweat and crowding, a farre worse stinck
than the ill formed Beasts they persecute with their dogs
and whips, Pick-pockets, which in an age are not heard of in
any of our Houses, repairing thither, and other disturbers of
the publike peace, which dare not be seen in our civill and
well-governed Theatres, where none use to come but the
best of the Nobility and Gentry; and though some have
taxed our Houses unjustly for being the receptacles of Harlots, the exchanges where they meet and make their bar-
gaines with their tranck chapmen of the Country and City,
yet we may justly excuse our selves of either knowledge or
consent in these lewd practices, we having no propheticke
soules to know womens honesty by instinct, nor commission
to examine them; and if we had, worthy were these wret-
ches of *Bridewell*, that out of their owne mouthes would
convince themselves of lasciviousnesse : Puppit-plays, which
are not so much valuable as the very musique betweene each
Act at ours, are still up with uncontrolled allowance, witnesse
the famous motion of *Bell* and the *Dragon*, so frequently vi-
sited at *Holbourne-bridge*; these passed Christmas Holi-
dayes, whither Citizens of all sorts repaire with far more
detriment to themselves then ever did to Playes, Comedies and Tragedies being the lively representations of mens
actions, in which, vice is alwayes sharply glanced at, and
punished, and vertue rewarded and encouraged ; the most
exact and naturall eloquence of our English language expressed and daily amplified ; and yet for all this, we suffer,
and are inforced, our selves and our dependants, to tender
our complaint in dolefull manner to you great *Phœbus*, and
you inspired *Heliconian* Virgins : First, our House-keepers,
that grew wealthy by our endevours, complaine that they
are enforced to pay the grand Land-lords rents, during this
long Vacation, out of their former gettings; in stead of ten,
twenty, nay, thirty shillings shares, which used nightly to
adorne and comfort with their harmonious musique, their
large and well-stuffed pockets, they have shares in nothing

with us now but our mis-fortunes; living meerly out of the stock, out of the interest and principall of their former gotten moneyes, which daily is exhausted by the maintenance of themselves and families.

For our selves, such as were sharers, are so impoverished, that were it not for some slender helps afforded us in this time of calamitie, by our former providence, we might be enforced to act our Tragedies: our Hired-men are dispertt, some turned Souldiers and Trumpetters, others destin'd to meaner courses, or depending upon us, whom in courtesie wee cannot see want, for old acquaintance sakes. Their friends, young Gentlemen, that used to feast and frolick with them at Tavernes, having either quitted the kin in these times of distraction, or their money having quitted them, they are ashamed to look upon their old expensive friends. Nay, their verie Mistresses, those Buxsome and Bountifull Lasses, that usually were enamoured on the persons of the younger sort of Actors, for the good cloaths they wore upon the stage, beleeving them really to be the persons they did only represent, and quite out of sorts themselves, and so disabled for supplying their poore friends necessities. Our Fooles, who had wont to allure and excite laughter with their very countenances, at their first appearance on the stage (hard shifts are better than none) are enforced, some of them at least to maintaine themselves, by vertue of their bables. Our boyes, ere wee shall have libertie to act againe, will be growne out of use like crackt organ-pipes, and have faces as old as our flags.

Nay, our very Doore-keepers, men and women, most grievously complaine, that by this cessation they are robbed of the priviledge of stealing from us with licence: they cannot now, as in King *Agamemnons* dayes, seeme to scratch their heads where they itch not, and drop shillings and half Crowne-pieces in at their collars. Our Musike that was held so delectable and precious, that they scorned to come to a Taverne under twentie shillings salary for two houres, now

wander

wander with their Inſtruments under their cloaks, I meane
ſuch as have any, into all houſes of good fellowſhip, ſaluting
every roome where there is company, with *Will you have
any muſike Gentlemen?* For our Tire-men, and others that
belonged formerly to our ward-robe, with the reſt, they are
out of ſervice : our ſtock of cloaths, ſuch as are not in tribu-
lation for the generall uſe, being a ſacrifice to moths. The
Tobacco-men, that uſed to walk up and downe, ſelling for a
penny pipe, that which was not worth twelve-pence an
horſe-load ; Being now bound under Tapſters in Inns and
Tippling houſes. Nay ſuch a terrible diſtreſſe and diſſoluti-
on hath befallen us, and all thoſe that had dependance on the
ſtage, that it hath quite unmade our hopes of future recove-
rie. For ſome of our ableſt ordinarie Poets, inſtead of their
annuall ſtipends and beneficiall ſecond-dayes, being for
meere neceſſitie compelled to get a living by writing con-
temptible penny-pamphlets in which they have not ſo much
as poetical licence to uſe any attribute of their profeſſion;but
that of *Quidlibet audendi?* and faining miraculous ſtories,
and relations of unheard of battels. Nay, it is to be feared,
that ſhortly ſome of them ; (if they have not been enforced
to do it already) will be encited to enter themſelves into
Martin Parkers ſocietie, and write ballads. And what a
Thame this is, great *Phœbus,*and you ſacred Siſters ; for your
owne Prieſts thus to be degraded of their ancient dignities.
Be your ſelves righteous Judges, when thoſe who formerly
have ſung with ſuch elegance the acts of Kings and Poten-
tates, charming like *Orpheus* the dull and brutiſh multitude,
ſcarce a degree above ſtones and forreſts into admiration,
though not into underſtanding with their divine raptures,
ſhall be by that tyrant Neceſſitie reduced to ſuch abject exi-
gents,wandring like grand children of old *Erra Peters,*thoſe
learned Almanack-makers, without any *Mecenas* to cheriſh
their loftie conceptions, proſtituted by the miſ-fortune of
our ſilence, to inexplicable miſeries,having no heavenly Ca-
ſtalian Sack to actuate and informe their ſpirits almoſt
confounded

confounded with ftupiditie and coldneffe, by their frequent drinking (and glad too they gan get it) of fulfome Ale, and hereticall Beere, as their ufuall beverage.

To conclude, this our humble complaint great *Phœbus*, and you nine facred Sifters, the Patroneffes of Wit, and Pro tectreffes of us poore difrepected Comedians, if for the prefent, by your powerfull interceffions we may be re-invefted in our former Houfes, and fetled in our former Calling, we fhall for the future promife, never to admit into our fixpenny-roómes thofe unwholefome inticing Harlots, that fit there meerely to be taken up by Prentizes or Lawyers Clerks; nor any female of what degree foever, except they come lawfully with their husbands, or neere allies : the abufes in Tobacco fhall be reformed, none vended, not fo much as in three-penny galleries, unleffe of the pure *Spanifh* leafe. For ribaldry, or any fuch paltry ftuffe, as may fcandall the pious, and provoke the wicked to loofeneffe, we will utterly expell it with the bawdy and ungracious Poets, the authors to the *Amtiodes*. Finally, we fhall hereafter fo demeane our felves as none fhall efteeme us of the ungodly, or have caufe to repine at our action or interludes : we will not entertaine any Comedian that fhall fpeake his part in a tone, as if hee did it in derifion of fome of the pious, but reforme all our diforders, and amend all our amiffes, fo profper us *Phœbus* and the nine *Mufes*, and be propitious to this our complaint.

FINIS.

TWO
ORDINANCES
OF THE
LORDS and *COMMONS*
Assembled in
PARLIAMENT

ONE

For the Lord Major of the City of *London, and the Justices of the Peace for the City,*
and parts adjacent, to suppresse Stage-
playes, Interludes, and common
Playes, and commit the Actors to
the Gaole, to be tryed at the next Sessions, to be punished as Rogues.

The Other

For setling of the Major, and Sheriffes, and
Establishing Officers for the City of
CHESTER.

And also for indempnifying of the Charter of the City.

Printed at *London* by *Robert Ibbitson,* in Smithfield,
neer the Queenes-head Tavern, 1647.

AN
ORDINANCE
OF THE
LORDS and *COMMONS*
Affembled in
PARLIAMENT
FOR
Setling of the Major, Sheriffes, and eftablifh-
ing Officers for the City of CHESTER.

Die Veneris 22 *Octob.* 1647.

WHEREAS the City of *Chefter*
hath been and continues grievoufly
infected with the Plague of Pefti-
lence, fo that the Citizens thereof could not
without inevitable danger affemble at the
ufuall time and place, to elect a Major, She-

A 2   riffes,

riffes, and other Officers of the said City, for this present yeare.

It is therefore Ordered and Ordained by the Lords and Commons in Parliament assembled, That *Robert Wright*, Alderman of the said City, shall be Major of the said City for this present yeare, untill the usuall time of Election, in the yeare 1648. according to the Charter of the said City. And that *William Wright*, and *Richard Minshall*, Citizens thereof; shall be Sheriffes of the same City, for this present Yeare untill the time aforesaid.

And the said Major shall take the severall Cathes which usually the Majors of that City at their Elections have taken, which shall be administred by *Christopher Bleafe*, Esquire, Alderman of the said City, and in his absence by the Eldest Alderman, resident in the said City. And the said Major having taken such Oathes, shall give to the said *William Wright*, and *Richard Minshall*, the severall Oathes which the Sheriffes of the said City, have usually taken at their Elections. And the said Major with the advice of the Aldermen

men and Common-councell, fhall upon the day of the taking their faid Oathes, make choyce of fuch other Officers for this prefent yeare, as are ufually Elected and chofen upon the election of Major and Sheriffes, and the faid *Robert Wright*, Major, fhall give unto the faid Officers fo elected and chofen, the Oathes ufually taken by fuch Officers.

And it is further Ordained, That the faid *Robert Wright*, *William Wright*, and *Richard Minfhall*, fhall be, and hereby are made Major and Sheriffes of the faid City, during the time aforefaid, to all intents and purpofes, as if they had been Elected at the ufuall time.

Provided, That this Ordinance, or any thing therein contained, fhall not for time to come, prejudice the Charter of the faid City, nor any of the Ancient priviledges, Liberties, and Immunities thereof.

Jo. *Brown*, *Cler. Parliamentorum.*
H. *Elfynge Cler. Par. Dom Com.*

A N

AN ORDINANCE

OF THE

LORDS and COMMONS

Aſſembled in

PARLIAMENT

FOR

The Lord Major of the City of *London*, and
the Juſtices of Peace, to ſuppreſſe Stage-
playes, and Interludes, &c.

Die Veneris, Octob. 22. 1647.

FOr the better ſuppreſsion of Stage
playes, Interludes, and common
Players.   It is this day Ordered by
the Lords and Commons in Parliament aſſembled, that the Lord Major
Juſtices of the Peace, and Sheriffes of
the

the City of *London* and *Westminster* ;
the Counties of *Middlesex* and *Surrey*, or any two or more of them, shall
and may, and are hereby authorized
and required to enter into all houses,
and other places within the City of
London, and Liberties thereof, and other places within their respective Jurisdictions, where Stage-playes, Interludes, or other common playes are,
or shall bee acted or played, and all
such common players, or Actors, as
they upon view of them, or any one
of them, or upon Oathes by two credible witnesses, (which they are hereby authorized to minister) shall bee
proved before them, or any two of
them, to have acted or played, in such
Play-houses or places abovesaid: and
all person and persons so offending, to
commit to any common Gaole or prison,

son , there to remaine untill the next
generall Sefsions of the Peace, holden
within the faid City of *London*, or Liberties thereof, and places aforefaid,
or fufficient fecurity entred for his or
their appearance at the faid fefsions.
there to be punifhed as Rogues, according to Law.

Jo. Brown, Cleric. Parliamentorum.

Hen. Elfynge Cler. Parl. Dom. Com.

FINIS.

AN
ORDINANCE
OF THE
LORDS and COMMONS
Assembled in
PARLIAMENT,

For,
The utter suppression and abolishing
of all
Stage-Playes
AND
INTERLUDES.

With the Penalties to be inflicted upon
the Actors and Spectators, herein exprest.

Die Veneris 11 *Februarii.* 1647.

ORdered by the Lords *Assembled in* Parliament, *That this
Ordinance for the suppression of Stage-Playes, shall be*
forthwith printed and published.

Joh. Brown Cler. Parliamentorum.

Imprinted at *London* for *John Wright* at the
Kings Head in the old Bayley. 1647.

Die Mercurii 9 *Februarii,* 1647.

AN ORDINANCE

For,

Suppreſſion of all Stage-Playes and Interludes.

Whereas the Acts of Stage-Playes, Interludes, and common Playes, condemned by ancient Heathens, and much leſſe to be tolerated amongſt Profeſſors of the Chriſtian Religion, is the occaſion of many and ſundry great vices and diſorders, tending to the high provocation of Gods wrath and diſpleaſure, which lies heavy upon this Kingdome, and to the diſturbance of the peace thereof; in regard whereof the ſame hath beene prohibited by Ordinance of this preſent Parliament, and yet is preſumed to be pra-

A 2   ctiſed

ctised by divers in contempt thereof. Therefore for
the better suppression of the said Stage-Playes, Interludes, and common Players, It is Ordered and
Ordained by the Lords and Commons in this present
Parliament Assembled, and by Authority of the
same, That all Stage-Players, and Players of Interludes, and common Playes, are hereby declared to be,
and are, and shall be taken to be Rogues, and punish-
able, within the Statutes of the thirty ninth yeare of
the Reigne of Queene *Elizabeth*, and the seventh
yeare of the Reigne of King *James*, and lyable unto the paines and penalties therein contained; and
proceeded against according to the said Statutes,
whether they be wanderers or no, and notwith-
standing any Licenfe whatsoever from the King or
any perfon or perfons to that purpose.

And it is further Ordered and Ordained by the
Authority aforesaid, That the Lord Mayor, Justices of the peace, and Sheriffs of the City of *London* and *Westminster*, and of the Counties of *Middlesex* and *Surrey*, or any two or more of them, shall,
and may, and are hereby authorized and required,
to pull downe and demolish, or cause or procure to
be pulled downe and demolished all Stage-Galleries.
Seates, and Boxes, erected or used, or which shall be
erected and used for the acting, or playing, or seeing
acted or plaid, such Stage-Playes, Interludes, and
Playes aforesaid, within the said City of *London* and Liberties thereof, and other places within
their respective jurisdictions; and all such common
Players, and Actors of such Playes and Interludes,

as

as upon view of them, or any one of them, or by Oath of two Witnesses (which they are hereby authorized to administer) shall be proved before them, or any two of them to have Acted, or played such Playes and Interludes as aforesaid at any time hereafter, or within the space of two Moneths before the time of the said Conviction, by their Warrant or Warrants under their hands and seales, to cause to be apprehended, and openly and publikely whipt in some Market Towne within their severall Jurisdictions during the time of the said Market, and also to cause such Offendor and Offendors to enter into Recognizance, or Recognizances, with two sufficient Sureties never to Act or play any Plaies or Interludes any more, and shall returne in the said Recognizance, or Recognizances into the Sizes or Sessions to be then next holden for the said Counties and Cities respectively; and to commit to the common Goale any such person and persons as aforesaid, as shall refuse to be bound, and finde such Sureties as aforesaid, untill he or they shall so become bound. And in case any such person or persons so Convicted of the said offence, shall after againe offend in the same kinde, that then the said person or persons so offending, shall be, and is hereby Declared to be, and be taken as an incorrigible Rogue, and shall be punisht and dealt with as an incorrigible Rogue ought to be by the said Statutes.

And it is hereby further Ordered and Ordained, That all and every summe and summes of Money gathered, Collected, and taken by any person or per-

sons

sons, of such persons as shall come to see, and be
Spectators of the said Stage-Playes, and Interludes,
shall be forfeited and paid unto the Church-wardens of the Church or Parish where the said summes
shall be so Collected and taken, to be disposed of to
the use of the poore of the said Parish, and shall
from time to time be leavied by the said Church-
wardens, and Constables of the said Parish, by Warrant under the hands and seales of any two of the
Justices of the Peace of the County, City, or Town
Corporate where the said summes are so taken and
Collected, upon complaint thereof to them made,
on the Goods and Chattels of the person or persons
Collecting the same, or of the person and persons
to whom the same shall be paid by them that Col-
lect the same, by Distresse, and sale of their Goods
and Chattels, rendring to them the overplus, upon
examination of the said persons, or proofe made
upon Oath before the said Justices of the summe or
summes so Collected and received, which the said
Justices are hereby authorized to take and examine.

And it is hereby further Ordered and Ordained,
That every person or persons which shall be present,
and a Spectator at any such Stage-play, or Interlude,
hereby prohibited, shall for every time he shall be
so present, forfeit and pay the summe of five shillings to the use of the poore of the Parish, where the
said person or persons shall at that time dwell or so-
journe, being convicted thereof by his owne con-
fession, or proofe of any one Witnesse upon Oath,
before

before any one Juftice of Peace of the County, City, or Towne-Corporate where the faid offence
is committed (who is hereby authorized to take the
fame Oath) to be leavied by the Church-wardens
or Conftables of the faid Parifh, by warrant of the
faid Juftice of Peace, by diftreffe and fale of the
Goods of the faid perfon offending, rendring to
him the overplus.

And it is hereby further Ordered and Ordained,
That all Mayors, Bayliffes, Conftables, and other
Cfficers, Souldiers, and other perfons being thereunto required, fhall be from time to time, and all
times hereafter, aiding and affifting unto the faid
Lord Mayor, Juftices of the Peace, and Sheriffes, in
the due execution of this Ordinance, upon paine to
be fined for their contempt in their negleft or refu-
fall thereof.

Joh. Brown, Cler. Parliamentorum.

FINIS.